The Storm's Flora

For Arthur and Louie

The Storm's Flora

Laura Wainwright

Seren is the book imprint of
Poetry Wales Press Ltd.
Suite 6, 4 Derwen Road, Bridgend,
Wales, CF31 1LH

www.serenbooks.com
Follow us on social media @SerenBooks

ISBN: 978-1-78172-791-1

A CIP record for this title is available from the British Library.

The publisher acknowledges the financial assistance of the Books Council of Wales.

EU GPSR Authorised Representative
Logos Europe, 9 rue Nicolas Poussin, 17000,
La Rochelle, France
E-mail: Contact@logoseurope.eu

Cover artwork: 'Artichoke (1915)' by Reijer Stolk, rawpixel.com
Author photograph: Darrell Thomas

Printed in Bembo by 4Edge ltd, Hockley.

Contents

Meadowsweet Gin

'over the centuries there were reports that children with bunches of
meadowsweet in their rooms were found insensible in the morning [. . .]
and it was thought dangerous to fall asleep in a field of meadowsweet'

Like damp hay the distiller warned,
handing me a jar that could have contained
sweepings from a barn floor.

And yes why, I wondered, on my birthday
choose meadwort, hayriff – clairvoyant queen
of the reen, ditch and sodden meadow,

Lleu Llaw Gyffes' maligned bride –
to what they say is the saddest drink,
the most ruinous,

when there were vials of dried lilac, lotus,
passionflower, pink hibiscus and honeysuckle,
wild violet, clover and rose?

I unscrewed the lid and breathed
the laced field's queasy analgesia. Spiked,
I climbed like a child the sweetness of the stack.

Although I had arrived, footsore,
after forty years of journeying, I knew
this was no place to lie down and rest.

The Lavender Bed

'A sprig of lavender held in the hand or placed under the
pillow enables you to see ghosts' – *Derek Jarman*

In the earthy hours
a scent's silhouette
with blurred purple curves,
the blueish gait of a figure at dusk
who might be approaching
or walking away.

As a child, I was afraid
to pass, to brush by
a bush that nodded
with bodies, the crowding
bees' push,
their violet whine.

Song of the Stinking Iris

Find me in the shy places
where fern and ivy thrive, a curiosity

amid a covenant of vines and spores,
a butterfly the shades

of an old bruise, exquisitely splayed,
pinned to my tall stem.

Find me where the steely dogwood
branches carve up the sky.

Bury me in their shadow
like a bone, secretive, possessive,

my meat unstripped and left to spoil,
my marrow mottled sun.

Anemone Nemorosa

'The word "anemone" translates from ancient Greek to "windflower"
or "daughter of the wind". [. . .] The European wood anemone
(Anemone Nemorosa) closes its petals at night-time and before rain'

Wind stirred the curtain
until the ceiling, the floor

sloped green
with a stale-sweet scent

of long-unopened things:
envelopes addressed in

in a tangled hand,
old passwords scrawled on their backs,

a bracelet abloom
in the deep shade of its box.

Half-invented rooms
piled with yellowed guides

to dragonflies, birds and botanica,
Wildflowers of the Wayside and Woodland,

rolled-up drawings,
speckled-brown maps.

Then, a creeping cold:
Winter rains rising

soaking my knees
where I knelt – stumped

beside foxhole and fern
for how long I couldn't say

waiting for the storm's flora,
the wood anemones

to look me
in the eye.

Flood

On the first day, rain painted my lichened limbs, my sleeves were scales
of green then grey and coral blue.

The next day a wind came up, a squall. I lost a limb. It tore
like lightning, lay hinged and splintered in the grass.

On the third day, a woman walked by in hood and boots, holding
hands with a child.

On the fourth day, in the usual way, I gradually became
the dark; though sluiced soil stirred, swilled my bloated roots.

On the fifth day, nothing existed but the river.

On day six, strange freight lurched and snagged aground.

On day seven, I startled at my own reflection.

From my heights a raft of rooks cawed:

More

Din y Frân Dragonfly

After W. H. Davies's poem and Danny Kirwan's adaptation into song

'And when the roses are half-buds half-flowers
and loveliest the king of flies has come' – *W.H. Davies*

Darter, Emperor, Chaser.
You might be all or none of these
names for highs and fireworks.

Still, you've come down drowsy and disarming
at Din y Frân, your scarped armour
glancing off cliffs and walls

to rest on a rolled leaf ripe to fall brown
as cigar-paper, the accepting tree your own
sheltered garden, your last-standing sun-tower

in this ice-versed wind – a rare-coloured guest
settled there, a borrowed song returned
and trembling on my thawing fingers.

The Garden of Earthly Delights

And then he just stopped playing
for years:

a refrain never questioned,
a lack made lore

like the story of how my mother chose him
because he made her laugh

or of when, a child climbing
an elder tree in The Pant Mawr

beer garden, I swallowed an ice cube whole,
turned such a dreadful, deathly pale

in the distorted pause, fed-back,
the silence whined.

A Fender and his father's Framus,
strings dull and slackened,

unchanged so long
I thought my fingers smelt of blood.

And I remember when I couldn't write
or speak the language; how

suddenly the garden was too cold
to hold a pen or book; I became

all the traitorous musicians
my father never forgave

because they smashed and torched
their instruments

and I lay my ear
on the varnished curve

of a guitar, listening
for a song.

Upcycling

that old barstool he balanced on for painting,
its heavy oak hatched and spattered,
its legs wobbly as scotch.
I thought of war-time bicycles pedalled
uphill by faded, sped-up men.
I slathered it with turpentine, watched, light-headed,
the years distil and widen
like pupils in the dark, then weep and muddy:
the thawing permafrost of dwelling.
With every scrape of sharpened
metal, the grain returned,
in wood-cut waves and cirrus clouds,
settling on the sanded seat,
varnished to flawed walnut,
I made for home.

Hasp

a word hoarse
in my throat, a harp
in the dark aeolian mode,
each note, though known,
sang there is no key
no code nor combination
just this brass
this hinge
and rasp
of dragged
and deadlocked oak
the clasp
that then the hatchet
broke

The Luthier

On the coldest morning she could recall,
breath scrawled about the mourners,
who rubbed and shuffled,
while blue grass sparkled
around a sound-hole in the earth.

From down there came the frost's harmonics –
three silverish strings – singing:
lully, lulla, lullay,
sleep well my luthier,
you made such music yet didn't play.

Mulberry Tree: A Folk Song

Here we go round
these ivied grounds
morwydden Din y Frân
morwydden Dwn-rhefn
sea worms' silk at Southerndown
in search of the mulberry tree.

By walls, down paths
it trails its fruit
and plays its shade
and strings its roots
morwydden Din y Frân
morwydden Dwn-rhefn
but nowhere your mulberry tree.

Here we go round
these ruined grounds
morwydden Din y Frân
morwydden Dwn-rhefn
crab-apples sour at Southerndown
old home of a mulberry tree.

By walls, down paths
it trails its fruit
and plays its shade
and strings its roots
morwydden Din y Frân
morwydden Dwn-rhefn
but nowhere your mulberry tree.

Salt-apples sour at Southerndown
old home of the mulberry tree.

Salt-apples sour at Southerndown
old home of the mulberry tree.

Crow

For Charlotte Greig

Charlotte, will you let me sing
    or am I another crow, unknown,
come late

from the hooded wood
    to your four walls,
your open window? Myself

found like a dropped locket?
    Long-memoried mimic I may be
any number of shadows,

so canny
    I barely ruffle the curtains'
blue eggshell.

But my voice I know
    I can't disguise
as it carks

and rattles
    fragile through
your songs, your tales

of strife and strength
    I never meant
to murder.

The Observer's Book of Birds

All these dreams of birds.
All these bird-voices urging

write them down,
don't write them down.

I won't tell you this
but I will.

I'll be the raven who raps
three times on your window

the curlew
from Lynette's room,

the herring gull indifferent
to your packed lunch.

Nothing more boring than birds
and other people's dreams.

Was that what the Surrealists said?
But no Bird Superior here.

I see stonechats, skylarks and swallows
jackdaws and jays

robins, reed warblers, wrens,
bullfinches, buntings and buzzards,

barn owls
like the one that somehow slipped

down the chimney into our unlit stove
and feigned death

in my father's hands,
a charcoal phantom,

all the flyaway pages
of that faithful Observer's Book.

Close

After Wallace Stevens

Stevens offered me thirteen ways –
but they all end here. The first
day of December: a blackbird

in the close
by the children's school.
He skittered out of the hedge

in front of my car, like
a moth from a dark rattan shade,
with a fog-lit beak full of worms.

Perhaps it was the synchronicity
of Budd and Eno's 'The Chill Air'
through the speakers,

the bare dawn hawthorn,
tangled with whip-its,
dogshit and tossed cans.

The moment made
my eyes mist. I slowed
to a crawl. We all star

in our own films. But this
is all about the blackbird, I know,
all about him.

Día de los Muertos

After Leonora Carrington

Día de los Muertos. Day two.
At her kitchen table
in Colonia Roma, Leonora
slides slippery
egg for tempera
between long fingers,
contemplates a raided grave.

Not for her
albumen's prison,
its transparency,
but the alchemy
of a second, silken realm
of unborn beasts,
creatures unconceived

in her palm
flor de Muerto – marigold
of the midnight sun,
kindly oil lamp
of an anglerfish,
entrancing
as a wheel on fire.

Brimstone

For Robert Minhinnick

When stonecrop sparks
aligned like Aquarius
in the dune

their sulphur-yellow
was the broken odour
of rock struck,

halved smartly as an egg
in the limestone dust.
But no water-bearer

that day
when Ffynnon y Twyni
ran dry

only a fire-sign
to steer a painted ship,
my hand to the marram

and a Brimstone
fanning
the buckthorns' shade.

Pwll Melyn

A poem in the voice of Siôn ap Hywel

Believe what you wish.
My first thought was where
were all the birds –

those angels at the windows,
the abbey's eyes, my spies
in the eaves and the yews' and willows' cowls.

Here I was at last
– *guennol gwennel, hirondelle* –
returned from fought sleep

to Llantarnam,
where sunlight bloomed on strange stone
as if there were a God.

Believe this if you wish.
I am painted
by fate:

my throat bloodied,
my wings smelted to a curved blade
that sinks to an Usk tarn's floor.

Its banks that May were cheered
by marsh iris
melyn ar goch

coch ar felyn –
each year around the jaundiced water
our outraged flag.

Ballad of Mary Grant, Newport, November 17th

For Julian Hayman

'Betrayed are the living, betrayed the dead'
— *Vernon Watkins,* 'Ballad of the Mari Lwyd' (1939)

Shouts tonight on the street
where I fell by the doorstep
of one Mary Grant
of Baneswell.

Three men in dark uniform.
A gang running away.
Go home, scolds a soldier.
I am home, I say.

My two daughters had just lain down when
I heard the crowds coming up from town:
gun-smoke news of an election called
and bullet holes still
in the Westgate's walls.

But I stepped out, with my son at my side,
in the lull before the storm arrived:
some had rifles and bayonets.
Others hurled stones.
But the only blood I saw was my own.

Men in dark uniforms.
Men running away.
Go home, snarls a solider.
I am home, I say.

Ice in the cemetery and
on the road where I fell.
Somewhere a stray firework
for Mary Grant
of Baneswell.

Woman at St Mark's

Audible some days from my desk,
the church organ of St Mark's – its descending
scales and muted swells, piped
through stone and mortar, a wrong sharp,
foolhardy flat falling on the tuned ear,
lost on an unlistening city.

At four o'clock, I'm ready to leave.
Her shouts and *fucks* – shrill then guttural,
are agitated enough to draw me
to the window and part the blinds,
wondering if she could be another
patient, another number –

as we all are. I once in my own way
astray, longing for light to fail,
for the road to dissolve into a kind
of consecrated quiet. I see her
in the yellowing dusk, try to climb
the churchyard wall again and again.

Legs benumbed and not her own,
dropping the bottle over first,
gently, as if it were a child.
For ten minutes I stay, watching
that absent dedication to
the spinning cause. Where did she go?

At home, I look out at the pumpkins
my children carved – their ragged mouths
laughing and gurning, filling with a month's rain.

Uskmouth Orchids

are scrubland flares, scarce
I thought, but bold today

where the dust path drifts
past the power station,

the tallow tower of its chimney.
Fluted? I ask my architect father.

He adjusts his binoculars, *Marsh…*
No, Reed Warbler, I think…

throat flowering among lilac spires,
mauve-flecked cairns, pylon wires

wood-wind canes, bands of sparrows,
goldfinches like red-tipped arrows,

the Levels' overlaid plans
vanishing points in an upstairs window.

*Wait…*he says. We stop.
I realise we have waited

all our lives to come here
together, to this retreating edge –

where, at last, soft-tongued and rootless
a cuckoo,

that grey-winged orchid,
speaks.

Usk Miles

Once I thought I could outrun the Usk,
so sluggish its competing currents,
so still the rippled inverse lamps
of the old Town Bridge:

a childlike thrill to think
to thwart the river. I, an outlier
where rats and rabbits dashed
and goldfinches left me in bronze dust

with the Usk-Mile Swimmers
before war and water's phosphate taint,
its tide-bared hulls of weekly shops.

Those rash racers, men and women, teenagers
smiling, capped, cross-armed and burly
in nineteen thirties newsprint

bathing suits – the silt-smack
of vanishment
on their cold lips.

Allotment

I'll
  cut
  the old
    ties
    let
    their fibres
      fray
        you
        free
      branch
       and stem
         loosen
       lift
      the dead
      roots
    we'll
      watch
       soil
     slip
    through
    our fingers
     releasing
    slackening
 lightening
    thudding
      where earthworms
        surface
       purple
        and
        squirming
         after long
        hours
       of rain
        under
         a song
         thrush's
          piqued
          eye

River Roses

At Newport's Glebelands

HC grows graffiti around her door:
river roses with a petrol scent

burgeoning in audacious sprays,
shouted shapes. 'HC' – insignia

of an intersection
imagist, stealthy as the Usk evening

between motorway lights,
caught in the drift, the uprising mud,

the rattle of half-empty canisters,
the rumble of HGVs

crossing concrete bridges overhead.
HC, I'm sorry. This mural is mine.

Your school-book blooms and neon-pink stars
tag patterns in my head

when it is day, the sun too fierce
for April.

I know nothing
in this place is as it seems;

these lush fields
are airbrushed too

their stories metres
deep.

Last Wasp,

its familiar drone,
not the empty radio frequencies
of the bluebottle, not
the charitable knocking of the bee.
Helicopter above the house,
hungry, winged dog,
harrying the apple
not yet hollowed,
the damson rotting under
the tree, where I tried
planting spearmint and thyme,
sniffing my hair, burring
my skin or wanting
however briefly
to know me. Last wasp
of the year, like
the last drinker
at closing,
climbing
down
the glass
to drown.

She Dotes

'She dotes on what the wild birds say
Or hint or mock at, night and day'
– *Edward Thomas*, 'She Dotes' (1915)

Who are you but your most faithful friend
and enemy: little rouged rival to your

riled reflection, night-eyed and moulted
at the window, on and off

the handle, fretting your flaws? You have me
still foraging in pots and faults for grubs

of meaning, symbol or portent, some outrage
or augury, a North wind, from heaven's territory,

when I need only watch for the next flash
and scratch,

           another fuss of feathers
on the glass.

Beechmast at Coed Melyn

In a dry month it falls
open-mouthed, stiff-tongued
shingle of the wood it shifts,
rolls under my soles, splits and cracks
with the earth, the cemetery's sagging wall,
its subsided graves.

But the light here, the colours, not yet half-mast.

As usual I gather a few – squeeze the husks
in my fist hard enough to know
our shared strength, a fact of this false autumn,
the barbed sepals startling my skin.
When inside all is thrift-shop jewellery-box soft –
as a doe's ear might be
or as a robin's auburn down once was –
as it sifted seed from my hand.

Fabular

There was once
a ravenous man from the road
who made soup from a stone.

I've read you the story
every night this week –
our *cawl carreg,*
a rough recipe

sweet with sprigs
and roots,
the jostling apothecary
of the pot.

It's the dupe
that gets you:
the sham magic
of a meal you won't eat.

The hope held
in a stippled stone
like a lone trout
trembling against a chalk stream.

The tale I knew took
a crooked turn: a nail tossed
in a broth of rust.

So here's a stone, swilled
where the water rolls clear.
Yours tonight
for the journey.

Suite of Rust

'There does seem to be a kind of psychic shape to a house'
– *Leonora Carrington*

I. Scythe

Top-heavy and tall as a man
the Sussex scythe leans

against Gwentian stone –
weary reaper in a webbed corner

the gothic blade dimmed
and dimpled with rust

but the long snath still handsome,
the precise polished brown

of beechnuts harvested
in another life

spent swinging at Summer
swathes of grass and nettles

knapweed, maybe hawkbit
lady's bedstraw

in my grandfather's garden
at the foot of the Downs

and, before that, rye
and hay cut for other barns,

different soils
whiter and more friable

than this heavy clay,
the butterflies

fleeing
in airy shades.

II. Hooks

They got me in the end:
those repetitions

in the kitchen.
As long as I can remember

all kinds of iron
hooks for hanging,

a sickle-shaped swarf hook
dark and dangerous,

an oak-handled billhook
for layering hazels

in Dorset's flint fields
from the grandfather

who never returned
what he borrowed.

Yes, my father was afraid
of thieves

knowing his barn
with its shoe-string timber façade

was no fortress
and I did sometimes wonder

why my young friends
who came to play looked

so alarmed, their eyes rising
to the largest one of all:

the docker's hook
for hauling freight

that my father found at work
forgotten beneath the floorboards

of Cardiff's Duke of Wellington –
a reminder of a harbour

brought home,
its coal-black neck arched and rearing

as a cormorant's
in Tiger Bay.

III. Shears

Brambles like coiled barbed wire
thick as your thumb

in the sloping field beyond the garden
around the spring

where the sheep went to drink.
We knew from their cries and brays,

unusually shrill and insistent,
that one was snared,

struggling and cut off
from the flock,

a leg ligatured
or thorns like a hackle's tines

snagged in the grubby fleece
their grip deepening

if anyone approached
but then, it always seemed, miraculously

freed – the uproar unreal
the early mist rising

from the unburdened land,
our concern inconsequential

as those blunted farmer's shears,
their still, gaping blades.

Patinas

After August Strindberg's Celestographs

Copernicus couldn't make it up.
This sky-scholar
who knew the lens's lies; made stars
of words and found them wanting.

Arcturus? Artless.
Alpha Centauri? Second-rate.
Magician, Hanged Man, Fool –
he laid out his deck of plates,

felt the high in common ground,
found fate's fingerprint nebulae,
a deity's dirt, oxidising, spreading
as oil will or anemones

unfurling in the sun.

Offa Rex

Midnight is a kind of truce.
Disturbed earth, redolent
with Eliseg's rains. Stilled
spades. Powys owls obscure,

vigilant in the wood. A watcher too
I crouch in my boundary tower, count
pouches of stars, see a barley
harvest moon crown over the ridge:

a king's dinar, dark-minted,
casting its show *shahada*
over these lands, inverting faith
and tongues in dug pools.

There are no gods but these alone:
the stamp of gold. And mountains,
forests, rivers, vales from sea to sea
to sea.

Ziziros: A Suite

Kyprogeneia

After Sappho (trans Anne Carson)

Or Aphrodite,
born from the foam
your unfaithful translations:

a waterpark,
an offshore gas field,
a luxury hotel,

of infinity pools,
honeymoon suites.
That word:

I want
a child's hungry hand
on the spear

of a thistle
outside Dionysus's
ruined house,

the cranes' high risings
above giftshops
teeming with tat

and love's tokens,
those cool sea caves
almost sanctuaries

from a hard sun,
the stare
of the waves,

from pigments
too painful, too tempting
to name.

Ziziros: A travelogue

Ziziros they chant
ziziros ziziros
raucous in the heat

rocks' salt cataracts
beyond the pool's sunscreen soup
hooded crows panting

Zivania cooled
with mint lemon juice – who drinks
fire-water at noon?

the buffet a feast
of crooned dubious ballads
Come on Eileen

in-house sparrows
dine here for free, fly their scraps
to the cliff-top palms

wading out, a cloud,
dimmed waves, come the tide coaxes
see what else I hold

is saltwater birth
and fate? my bruised bloodied knee
the rocks' reminder

compelling this swell
but only the locals know
its submerged terrain

Loukoumi spectra
of the counter, yes both sides
claim these dusty jewels

street cat crouched under
the oleander, one ear
torn in the shade wars

a woman, two long-
tailed lizards on her shoulders
photo five euro

giftshops sell olives
ornate wooden penises
owls of Athena

scored into a seat
above the sea "life is porn"
a god's graffiti

Gods and beasts arrayed
in tiles and stones, on oiled skin
bared ink mosaics

looking for lizards
in the brittle scrub beer cans
wedding confetti

the sand hot ash,
stubbed cigarettes, a Clouded
Yellow butterfly

terebinth heavy
with human hopes outside
the kilned catacomb

a caved dry-stone wall
in and out lizards sprint like
us in the labyrinth

Ziziros they chant
ziziros ziziros
raucous in the heat

Jelly

Bloodless heart,
eyeless lens,
brain splayed, without circuitry,
its hemisphere of flies.
All these owned and unowned parts
are here in their hundreds
where I hunt for shells, half-whole,
stones that look like moons;
a retreated wave made flesh,
a coroner's calm. They say

one day the sea will heat,
shed its scales, boil
all its claws, its teeth and bones,
to gelatine.
I see a red star, setting;
a mirage in a mould.

On the mood-enhancing benefits of sea-swimming

'"Aquatic life is bathing in a soup of anti-depressants" says marine biologist'

Serotonin swells
       the shock of euphoria

which is early asphyxia
       or how we drown

how seawater wrests
       your breath clamps

your throat tight
       as a dredged shell

then the beating abates
       and you begin to feel

a sense of calm
       of indifference or apathy

peculiarly warm
       neither pleasure

nor distress
       while neural networks

of weed
       you once thought the skirts of jellyfish

graze your thighs
       caress your fingertips

the lapped nape of your neck
       their every stroke

simulating yours
     as you fix your lips

against each lift and fall
     scull further

and further
     from who you thought

you were

Night Vision Suite

I. Swimmer/*Nofiwr*

After the painting by Graham Sutherland in the National Museum of Wales

Sutherland's swimmer glides through green water, not a splash
but a wave

mid-stroke across the bedroom wall

nofiwr y nos, Sutherland's swimmer

floods my sleep with dreams

I am krill, girl and seal / koi, porpoise and boy

unborn, weightless, arms and legs finning

towards a shore of shucked forms far as the midnight zone

where Sutherland's swimmer, dives in jade water, not a splash
but a wave

II. Night Vision

Trying to settle,
      I'm dust disturbed,
sleet
      on a salted road.

When he wakes, I stroke his hair,
      say in my calmest
maternal voice: *close your eyes,*
      breathe,
picture a peaceful scene.

Tonight, I take my own advice,
      visualise a simple stone house
against a slope of heather,
      a track down to a copse of rose-gold beech,
a rattling, bell-clear stream.

Inside, there's an unguarded fire,
      a deep and drowsy chair
where I sit. Through a window,
      I watch a bleary day-moon
make an icon of my words: *there,*
      you see?
The world stays just the same when it gets dark.

III. Noctua

A laundry huff of air,
a weight kneading my shoulder,
testing a left nest.

An owl has shaken me
from a long wakefulness;
her wing sweeps my ear.

I am floored, but follow the track
with the assurance of a falconer.

Trees are lithographs in the hollowing light.
Last week's snow is peeling on the hills like old paint.

What has to die tonight?

When, with ungainly grace,
the owl has gone, brief as a flower,
I scan the needled taupe.

I miss her painfully, like birdsong
though she left me a capsule of odd bones.

Cinquain for a Marked Tree

Tree, you
art sick they say;
your body blained silver
and blue-whealed: your harmonious
dis-ease.

Help Lines

The caller was afraid to go home.
I'm in the woods.
I panicked and hid here.
A voice intimate and exiled,
slight as the silver birch,
or the hazels dripping that March
with catkins – yellow green,
a running colour.

I said what I was trained to say:
Don't talk to them.
Don't let them in.
Leave nothing valuable on view.
And if you have a car,
park it two or three streets away

On the road perhaps where, walking
one year later, I tried to save
an injured bird. Wide-eyed starling
with a crimped wing – tormented
by two magpies, plunging and swiping,
their raucous demands:
the hammering of fists
on a door

Sertraline

'fruit, which, tasted once, must thrall me here'
– *Dante Gabrielle Rossetti*, 'Proserpine'

Such devotion you demand,
Sertraline – parched prayer
on the tongue, on the palm
benign as a pomegranate seed.

Believe *me*:
when I say your name I see
a goddess, with red hair, then umber,
as Rossetti painted Proserpine

in his own nervous hell.
I think now we are one mind.
One flesh. Your half-life
bisecting mine.

And like Proserpine,
your reluctant half-sister,
I can never leave
the unlit land for long.

The Air

Now a spot of warm rain
earths amongst the static grasses
where ragwort masses,
dwarfing orchids:

its ragged yellow
towering, buzzing like pylons,
the crickets' voltages invisible

as when, near the power station,
we stop under heavy wires,
beside the spikes and lightning-bolt signs,

say, can you hear it?

Not the thunder over the sea
or that childhood night-shock
of animate metal

but everywhere and nowhere,
the thrumming air
powering the swifts' and dragonflies'
trajectories,

the tinnitus
of this lengthening year.

Addendum

Here and there I will leave you
a sign.

Something inscrutable.
A coincidence

ordinary and aslant,
dismissible

as news
from an unvisited country.

Know everything
at first will be an omen

and your glasses useless
in such stumbling light.

So lace your stiff boots
and put on my coat,

always too big,
the sweet mulch

of me
done up to your throat.

We saw many autumns
though none

in this place.

Teasels

After found materials sent by artist and ceramicist, Kim Norton

No teasing them from this matted ground.
To try is to taste the pylons' metal,
to glimpse the goldfinch's crimson mask
on your palm.

Today they card and comb a slow drizzle;
a mist shorn from clay-bone waves,
its nap scented with salt and dung
and the Severn's industrial breath.

Once I cut five tough stems,
positioned each spiny sea-urchin bloom
in a vase precisely as the Teasel Man
at his gig.

Cogs of lost summers
they work on, softened, disentangling light
and shadow, the days settling between each thorn
in a pale pollen.

Towards Marros Sands

*Composed using words, images and materials sent by artist
and papermaker, Jane Ponsford*

bramble gorse fern
and all the way
and over us
the hanging strata

of stone
falling
footholds
a path unsound
sounding

all the way
the evening
steepening
bramble earth fern
gorse earth stone

the sea below
slick as slate
holding the light
all the way
and over us
dark gold

the gorse aurora

Asterisms

'...of what man-made echo does the mind not weary,
as it turns endlessly round the Earth?'
– *Vernon Watkins*, 'Aphorisms' (1960)

★
★   ★

What Holi clouds beyond this blindfold.

What shining dust.

Brittlestar.

Algae, anemone, capillary.

Pathogen, damselfly.

All returned. Ferociously, obliviously elegised.

Patterns disarray, redraw.

Scales tilt.

Colours scumble and phase.

Wildfires devour themselves, take an ice age to reach you.

This silence is the loudest sound you'll never hear.

Yours are lightning years.

Other coordinates.

Notes

Meadowsweet Gin
Quotation from Rosamund Richardson, *Britain's Wild Flowers* (London: National Trust Books, 2017), p. 179.

Lleu Llaw Gyffes is a figure from the *Mabinogi,* a collection of Welsh medieval tales. A magician made him a wife, Blodeuwedd, out of flowers.

The Lavender Bed
Quotation from Derek Jarman, *Modern Nature* (London: Vintage, 1991), p. 55.

Song of the Stinking Iris
'Stinking Iris' – *Iris Foetidissima.* Its leaves give off a smell of roasted or rotten beef when torn or crushed.

Anemone Nemorosa
Quotation from Sally Coulthard, *Floriography: The Myths, Magic and Language of Flowers* (London: Quadrille, 2021), p. 63.

Din y Frân Dragonfly
Din y Frân is a Welsh name for Dunraven, Vale of Glamorgan, used by Iwan Llwyd in Iwan Llwyd and Aled Rhys Hughes, *Rhyw deid yn dod miwn* (Llandysul: Gomer, 2008), p. 104.

W.H. Davies's poem, 'The Dragonfly' (1927), was adapted by musician, Danny Kirwan. His song, 'Dragonfly', was recorded and released as a single by Kirwan's band, Fleetwood Mac in 1970. Kirwan left the band in 1972. Quotation from the song and the original poem.

Mulberry Tree: A Folk Song
This song incorporates two Welsh names for 'Dunraven' and the Welsh for 'mulberry tree'.

Crow
Charlotte Greig (1954-2014) was a folk musician and writer who lived in Wales for a number of years. 'Crow' echoes her songs, 'Crows', 'Trees' and 'Go from my Window', which can be found on the albums, *Night Visiting Songs* (1998 and 2023), *Down in the Valley* (1999) and *Quite Silent* (2005) respectively.

The Observer's Book of Birds
This poem echoes Lynette Roberts's 'Curlew' (1944).

Close
'The Chill Air' can be found on Brian Eno and Harold Budd, *Ambient 2: Plateaux of Mirror* (1980).

Día de los Muertos
The Mexican 'Day of the Dead'.
'*Flor de Muerto*' – the symbolic marigold or 'flower of the dead'.

Brimstone
Ffynnon y Twyni – Welsh, meaning 'Well in the Dunes' (also known as 'Burrows Well'), Merthyr Mawr Dunes, Bridgend County.

Pwll Melyn
Welsh – 'yellow pool'.

Siôn (John) ap Hywel – Cistercian Abbot of Llantarnam, was a soldier and spiritual leader in Owain Glyndŵr's army. He rallied the troops on the banks of the Usk during the Battle of Pwll Melyn, Usk, on 5th May 1405. Glyndŵr's army was defeated and Siôn ap Hywel killed.

'Gwennol, gwennel, hirondelle' – Welsh, Breton, French for 'swallow'.

Marsh iris – also known as 'yellow flag iris'.

Ballad of Mary Grant, Newport, November 17th
Mary Grant (aged 52) and her young son, Charles, were bayonetted to death in peace time during political rioting in Newport in 1868, at the hands of British soldiers. A jury returned a verdict of accidental death. Mary and Charles were buried in an unmarked grave in St Woolos Cemetery, Newport. Their grave remains unmarked today.

Usk Miles
The inaugural Usk Swim in Newport was held in 1912. The event was stopped in 1938 because pollution in the river was considered too high. For more information, see: https://www.southwalesargus.co.uk/news/17934645.swimmers-raced-river-usk-newport/

River Roses
The Glebelands is an area of contaminated land in Newport that has been turned into parkland and playing fields. For more information, see: https://www.southwalesargus.co.uk/news/4087661.newport-recreation-ground-closed-after-toxic-find/ and https://www.chepstowfoe.org.uk/glebelands/abt_glblnds.htm

This poem draws on the following lines from 'Sea Rose' (1916) by HD: 'more precious than a wet rose single on a stem – you are caught in the drift'.

Beechmast at Coed Melyn
Coed Melyn (Welsh) – 'yellow wood'. Located in Allt-yr-yn, Newport.

Fabular
'Cawl cerrig' – Welsh, 'stone soup'.

Suite of Rust
Quotation from an interview with Leonora Carrington in the BBC documentary, *Leonora and the House of Fear* (1992).

Offa Rex
See the gold dinar of King Offa in the British Museum.
Eliseg was ruler of Powys, Wales, during the 8th century.

Kyprogeneia
Cypriot name for the goddess, Aphrodite, and used by the poet Sappho. The poem draws on Anne Carson's translations of Sappho in *If Not, Winter* (London and New York: Virago, 2003).

Ziziros: a travelogue
'Ziziros' (Greek Cypriot) – cicada
Zivania – traditional Cypriot alcoholic drink made from grape skins
Loukoumi (Greek) Lokum (Turkish) – Turkish delight

On the mood-enhancing benefits of sea-swimming
Headline taken from: https://bigthink.com/life/what-are-dangers-eating-seafood/

Sertraline
Quotation from Dante Gabriel Rossetti, 'Proserpine' (1880), a translation of the Italian sonnet inscribed on his painting of the same name.

Towards Marros Sands
Marros Sands, Carmarthenshire.

Acknowledgments

Versions of some of these poems have previously been published in *Air and Armour* (Green Bottle Press, 2021), *Coedcernyw – among other things* (Clutag Press, 2023) and *Thrall: Poems and Art* (Seventh Quarry Press, 2025), a collaboration with poet, Robert Minhinnick.

Versions of some of these poems have also appeared in *Magma, Poetry Wales, Poetry Birmingham, Litmus Magazine, Anthropocene* and *The Seventh Quarry Magazine.*

'Offa Rex' was commissioned by visual artist, Dan Llywelyn Hall, for his 2021 exhibition, *Walking with Offa/Cerdded gydag Offa*' and published in the book, *Walking with Offa/Cerdded gydag Offa* (Ravenmade, 2021). 'Pwll Melyn' was written for Dan Llywelyn Hall's more recent artistic project, '*Llys Glyndŵr*' and published in *Llys Glyndŵr: A Creative Response to the Lives of Owain Glyndŵr's Supporters* (Ravenmade, 2025).

An earlier version of 'River Roses' was commissioned by the environmental charity, Sustainable Wales/*Cymru Gynaliadwy* and published in Robert Minhinnick (ed), *Gonvelion: Shared Horizons* (Parthian, 2021).

An earlier version of 'Uskmouth Orchids' was written for Sustainable Wales and first published in *A Newport Journal,* available at: https://www.sustainablewales.org.uk/a-newport-journal-index

An earlier version of 'Usk Miles' featured in the *Afon Wysg/River Usk* art exhibition at Cwtsh Community and Arts Centre, Newport, in 2025.

'Teasels' and 'Towards Marros Sands' originated from a collaborative project with visual artists, Kim Norton and Jane Ponsford, in association with Oriel Myrddin, Carmarthen.

I am very grateful to Zoë Brigley and Rhian Edwards, poetry editors at Seren, for their help in refining and shaping this collection.

Thank you always, Darrell Thomas, for your love and support.

About the author

Laura Wainwright was born in Cardiff and grew up in Newport, Gwent, where she still lives. She attended school in Newport and Cardiff University where she obtained a BA, MA and PhD in English Literature. Her PhD thesis focused on Anglophone Welsh literature and was later published as *New Territories in Modernism: Anglophone Welsh Writing, 1930-1949* by the University of Wales Press. Laura has also published poetry pamphlets, *Air and Armour* (Green Bottle Press, 2021) – the outcome of a Literature Wales Writer's Bursary – and *Coedcernyw: among other things* (Clutag Press, 2023). *Thrall: Poems and Art*, a collaboration with Robert Minhinnick featuring Laura's poetry and artwork, was published in February 2025 by Seventh Quarry Press.